Grunt Work

Sounds from Everyday Living

Heather Finton

published 2017 by Northern Undercurrents

ISBN 978-0-9958247-6-8

cover artwork by Bee Smyth

As your spirit

says hello

in everyday now

may your heart be soft

and your mind

free enough

to chuckle.

Let me draw you in
with the feel of breeze
in a cool sunlight,
travelling birds without names
making melody
over percussive rustling,
like ocean
only more grounded.

Sit in the too-much of it,
the way the leaves let wind
stretch them in full exuberance,
pulling them off any pretense of
balance
full green knowing
it is not the season to fly.

Take off your sweater
even though you still need it,
let the inner warmth
be enough
even as wind carries it elsewhere.

Freedom is always instant,
the way pollen only flies now,
only lands once,
sounds collective
but only nurtures in the singular,
and not tomorrow.

He stood
beside a pile of socks,
most of them with holes

and spoke the desolate query,
wanting a meaning of life.

She did not run or soothe
but stood near,
stark silence
falling like hail,
making room for cold.

And spoke her joy,
the way that spruce needles fall
making lie of evergreen,
the way vacuum is traversed
by globes of fire
at impossible distance,
the truth of each bag of cells
held long enough
to make a lifetime.

His hands fluttered
more than once that day,
brushing aside her words,
dandruff in a snowstorm.
And flakes still swirl
around them both,
the smile and sigh of it.

My husband
sings to me in Sanskrit
before dawn
and rises from our bed
to make kale smoothies
by hand
so the blender won't rouse the kids.

We sip
in starlight
savouring life
and practicing Japanese
while we do yoga
and shower with natural oils,
enjoying tantric thrills
before shared letter-writing
for Amnesty
and a practiced review of our balance
sheets.

Our green home
leaks no heat
and keeps us warm,
well-watered
for cooking all organic meals,
parenting with the tongues of angels.

Perhaps it is true
that fiction poisons,
clouds the clear water
of what is here
and giving life.

My true vocation
is to savour,
to read with eyes
that see the glow
rising inside,
touched by fibres
conveying nutrition.

There is reluctance
in the yin,
the vocation as reader,
receiving as audience,
one among many.

And also a smile
rising from belly,
the useless power
of a sand speck
settling in,
jostled by neighbours
to create this fertile soil
simply
because we are here.

Robust trust,

like a matriarch

tapping her foot

in a room where she has stood

largely ignored

and fully present,

grounded and slightly grumpy

even as she extends warm arms…

like a colony of ants

churning earth

one grain at a time,

small clumps of life

rearranged

to make corridors for living,

foundational enterprise

invisible and ongoing…

like the smooth black

of a wiped slate,

computations erased,

exchanged for clarity,

a nothingness that contains,

a moistened sponge.

Public Consultation

So many ears have stopped listening
as if the words are just labels
for sorting on jars
and stacking somewhere, unnoticed.

What would you do
if the sweet spruce
and campfire smoke
mingled with crackling
told your ears something new?

What would you do
if those real soundings
deeper than words
welcomed your feet
on kinnikinnick ground
made of the same cells you breathe?

What if your place
at the top of the earth
called a warning
and begged for cherishing?

My friend has worked for years
listening to the caribou people
and with those who measure carefully
— she made a book
filled with wisdom,
a beautiful book I only glanced at.

My gift is not with numbers
but I trust the ones
that add up to subtraction,

the math that says we're losing
if we don't change.

My own changing
has been slow and urgent both,
my song of movement
is shared by many,
not only a lament
but a deep invitation
to move the way you are meant to
in caring for what is still here.

- Northern Cardinal Review 2014

Wink

The truth is,

this morning some of my first thoughts

were of my mortgage

and how I am not grown up enough

to understand capital gains

and how I fear the games

involved in appraisals.

And as I stumbled towards coffee,

the mountains winked,

and a million aspen leaves were waving

and I came so very close

to missing their greeting

and not waving back.

Chitter

We look at ducks

or squirrels

and know they are alive

doing what they do

as part of the biosphere

and cosmic dance.

The sun

looks down on us

with the same warm certainty.

We who get confused about God

and think we must carry

all this creation

can also settle back

in our own splashing,

chittering our gratitude,

sensors for consciousness

living now.

Sometimes truth
feels like a new wing
sprouting from my heart;
ungainly, flapping hard
so I feel breeze,
lopsided and tender.

In this way
I am not flying
but trace
with wondering fingers
the bones and feathers
of a wing I never saw before.

Your sad scraping
at the illusion we call life
has been such a deep gift.

What I in blindness saw
as impediment to living
has been my doorway in;
all those anguished questions
let me scrape my own heart
to this bare joy.

Without your harsh lessons
I would have whistled forever in
darkness,
smiling in my sleepy state.

And now my precious grin
flows from this raw knowing
that even darkness embraces,
that light and shadow
play across the land,

that nothing is wasted
ever
even as we drowse our days
under flickering skies.

This wing
is only new to my knowing,
has been part of my shape
waiting for discovery,
will someday ride currents,
implied precision and balance
growing by design.

Hot Potato on the Couch

When I sit here
and pat the universe
in my belly

and catch myself wanting
to be the queen bee

I pay homage
to all the other worker bees
like me,

the wisdom-tenders
in their many seats,
galaxies of wonder
unnoticed and connected.

This couch potato
in such a small sphere
does not need Oprah
for proclaiming wonder,
does not need proclamations
to feel the heat,
to know that life is here,
to feel the way we are cooking
even as it looks like nothing moves.

Mistress

There is a place
beyond doubt

where meaning speaks so clear
that purpose is obvious
even as it makes no sense

artists splashing their detritus on walls
hailed as beauty or junk
- opinion
so secondary
to the primacy of the call

urgency
of the life force rising

the kunda demanding allegiance
from pen or clay or spices

a flow beyond reason
like a dance mistress
thumping her stick
on the floor,
terrible and true
in making movement.

Tonight the goddess
has crossed her arms
and taps her foot,
impatient with me
and my load of excuses.

Her sword slices,
my burdens diminished,
me still clinging
as if the papers
mean something,
as if I can avoid her gaze.

Such love,
rupturing the membranes
where I linger,
air rushing into my lungs
like a new food,
nurturing.

Wet and fragile, yes,
but breathing
as if this element were mine,
as if I was crafted
for this sustenance.

This nurturing dive
like dropping in to breasts
or bread dough
or a billowing trampoline

secure in the unknown landing
and flung beyond control.

A chemistry of yeast and patience,
time essential
in the rising

feeling how time
is a malleable ingredient,
kneaded and stretched.

Tendrils of past and future
inevitably feed this now,
capillaries of story
being told.

Enveloped by soft nothing,
we fly and fall,
blanket-tossed
by seen and unseen friends.

You have two brothers
and after all this time
they are my family too.

Between us we have
these blurred edges
where we sing different songs
and share many harmonies.

Between us we pass the stories
back and forth,
sometimes to get them out of our hands
like hot potatoes,
sometimes to transfer
precious pearls.

It is too easy to say
that your brothers' dramas
are just their own,
too easy to say that they are here
in your story
as separate from mine,
too easy to say that somehow
I have conjured up this discomfort to
teach me.

A braver thing
to find freedom
inside these blurred convergences.

Bouncing off the walls
and the floor,
I'd hit the ceiling
if I could,
or scratch my claws in it

rub my fur the wrong way
either way

feeling my gloss
turn to mange
as static lifts it,
hairs on end
and buzzing.

Hardly invitation,
I'd like some petting
but see how my hiss and spit
tell a different truth

know this agitation
will burn itself out,
a patch of sunlight
find in me a bed.

I wish I could share
the space before the poem,
cool empty where nothing
IS
so brightly,
whispers of words
on the edges of it,
meaningless and loved.

Like a penny dropping
in place
except not at all the same,
or taking off a cloak
so it slides to the floor,
marking a perimeter
completely permeated.

And words
like precious baubles
spill their breadcrumbs,
pointing and feeding,
playing out a trail
that circles inwards
home.

I kiss galaxies
from this couch
and frolic with dolphins
and pay bills in my head
and send loving letters
that never reach the mailbox

and feel the divine wave
as I couch-surf in one place

and wonder what happens next

but I sit here
with the feel of worn fabric

until movement
is obvious.

Even when I'm hooked
it's not the end of the world;
we all get stabbed by the needle
and it is just a way
of making doilies,
of being crafted,
divine crochet.

We can help
by not grasping at the hooks,
letting ourselves be poked
and shaped into new holes
like spiderwebs and snowflakes
and beautiful open artwork,
pointless handcrafts
of an unseen maker,
intricate, unique,
unravelled
time and again.

All these birds:
some that huddle
in their nests
afraid to fly;

some that follow the leader
and go the distance,
thousands of miles
journeyed in precision,
lifted by the wind on other wingtips;

some that practice flight
only enough to eat
and catch a wafting breeze,
an invitation to pause
and sometimes be carried
on a rising thermal,
circling with no effort.

Letting God Break My Hip

I feel like there's a showdown planned
for soon,
the kids are texting
for a fight,
a gathering on the playground,
me against God.

Or the goddess
whose blurred faces
wave sleepily
when I'm unfairly dozing.

It's not a fight I can win,
am vanquished already
but some part is still
balling her fists

yelling "show yourself"
to the dark

angry at all this waiting,
these self-induced nosebleeds,
the ring of unseen watchers
I perform for.

In some versions
of the dark night
there is caress
in the cracking of the joints,
a tangible touch
despite the pain.

For a long time
I wanted to be held tenderly

and even as I stand here lonely,
clenched hands shaking,
some part under my feet
knows the bullpen
is enclosed,
the matador will not visit,
the flowers still keep falling,
petals crushed and beautiful.

My deepest fears
are the most ridiculous

am speechless for so long
around my fear of flaming,
burning all I love
with my powerful light

my fear of cold and wet
as if it is a secret shame
that no one shares

my fear of loss
and the puncture of love's sword
to leave me crippled,
bereft of all protection

and yes,
my fear of death,
inescapable touch,
a worm wiggling early
against the hook that will come
instead of burrowing
in the feel of earth.

My coffee pot
sounds like an old man coughing
and I feel like it is telling me
something about love

abrupt, short-lived,
unusual, trying to wake me up

like the elder
who told me to pay attention
when you see a bird or beast
out of its normal range

and I feel the stillness
of my listening

and the empty questions
dropping like husks

no answers

arousal rising
as response
to sun on leaves
briefly green.

Descending clarity
falls like a smooth pond,
sliding down my head and heart
to land on my hips
like an unruffled tutu,
the bustle weighty and balanced.

Not certainty,
not entire ease,
leaving room for my preferred tensions
and these patterns of holding,
the pond wets the moment
by moving outwards
to touch unseen shores
in all directions.

My drinking straw
runs through me,
there is no need to sip;
water flows
because it does,
because sometimes it does.

This pen
is not a life raft
nor a polaroid
or even a paddle
but just an extension of my hand,
outstretched in invitation.

Leopard

I see the flick
of a leopard's tail
swishing with frustration,
gazing from a supple branch
as I scurry,
avoiding her stare.

She twitches
and growls,
ready to pounce

wanting to leap
beyond my tight circles

some part of me
feels her soft fur
and irritation,
ready to stretch

may she find freedom
in her bounding,
release in instinct,
a landing on unseen ground.

I'll show you mine
if you show me yours

and here's the rub
… somehow I want yours
as an offering,
want you to say what you're showing,
want you to seem awake
while you share
your rumpled treasures,
want you to tell me what you know
or don't know
so I can play too.

And maybe I just don't get it;
maybe there is no need
to play by these rules;
maybe the showing is wordless,
maybe the silence that holds us
is the good kind.

Like a kid
in an ice cream parlour
where they let you taste
all the flavours

I want you beside me
and want to give you spoons
and want to watch you try
all this pleasure

and there is nothing wrong
but it is a little weird
and does get in the way
of my own savouring.

So much joy
right here under glass
and free for the asking,
and my voice has a
practiced quaver
but I am starting to laugh at it.

Yes, I want more spoons
than a good girl should,
and look how my curiosity propels my
lovely greed,
how I sample
this multilayered buffet,
the cold sweet.

Solar cell

I need to scoop light
each day,
feeling atoms wiggle,
evaporating residue,
recharging luminosity.

Even on the days
I see only clouds
or feel the slap of cold rain,
particles of light
still shimmer unseen
to fuel me.

No searching,
no quest,
a simple act
of opening.

My lady blue
pale and piercing
swirls skyward with ease
curving benediction downwards
not as blanket
but elixir

this spacious love
connecting tides and stars
released from gravity
like a light beyond speed,
descending by choice
to caress
her cousin Gaia

a sky-goddess laughing at the sun
and juggling several

too long forgotten
by her daughters,
borne in their bellies.

Baby Steps

Until you know
how to craft a galaxy
with lifetime in it,
you can pretty much assume
that all your paces
are baby steps.

Which may sound useless
except for the joy
in real babies,
how they stagger
and fall
with tears
and shrieks of delight,
victorious
at the edge of their beginnings,
expanding realm.

So much kindness today,
the universe
sending me roses,
and me still wanting more.

In fact all day
people keep offering love
and I keep saying thanks
with my mouth
or hugs or tears
and still gape
like a stupid fool
at a store window,
wanting what is out of reach.

It's hard to complain
about such a lovely story
and still I twist the edges
to favour distortion,
imagine an itch
no fingers can scratch,
mastering dissatisfaction
with well-honed skill.

Let this be more than a wallow,
let my shit
enrich some future growth;
may this whining resonate
a warning,
provoke some startled leap.

Band-aids

All those times
my band-aids stick
and I offer them up
to your bleeding

you think I have no wounds,
I wander the battlefield unscathed,
some lost Pollyanna
out of touch
with the reek of madness,
the stench of all this decay.

I have lain here
in the mud,
my friends dead
beside me,
parts missing,
grieving amputated limbs
and letting muck
bathe stumps in festering;

felt cold wet excremental days
try to drown me
in paralysis,
staring at the sky
that pours rain and snow
on my clammy skin.

Don't talk to me of innocence;
I have lived too deeply
for too long
to feel like the movie set
where I wander in comfort
is a true place

meet me instead
on the charnel ground
and if I hand you
a band-aid
let its symbol
touch beneath your sneering,
find a little grace
to see from where it comes.

Bracelet

Moving in dreamtime,
awake with warm sunshine
and the old lady coughing on the porch

I wear this symbol of waiting
for love and return

letting it encircle
my wrist
holding an open palm

the way I am tempted always
to cling
but don't need to

the way there is yearning
singing me alive

barely soothed
but still here

encircled
and curious

moved by the sight
of my own graceful bondage

helpless and healing.

with thanks to B&J

36

All the fixes
scratched in sand,
goals and intentions
briefly on display
at water's edge,
soon illegible.

Meaning shoved aside
for its profound cousin,
unintelligible
but vaguely sane,
honouring the feel of water,
the flash of golden flecks
on willing toes.

I can barely imagine
the ants in my own yard
let alone my continent
or all of them,

or even a billion kids
in primary schools.

My promises are small,
wrapped around the stature
of my days,
hoping to let light penetrate,

alchemy of time and water.

Nothing Happens Next

Fingers that flinch
and no longer lie flat
without effort, curled in receiving.
Despite all this building
and trying to fix,
planting
and waiting for fruit,
designing
a pattern to be sewn

nothing happens next,
there is no
sweet resolution,
happy someday

just a slow crawl
towards a deeper sit
an open hand
uplifted fingers
greeting what is here.

There are certain views
I've been avoiding,
like the stretch marks
on the underside of my thighs
I rarely notice
except in postures
where my nose sniffs
at the distance to the ground.

The lines run
like old lava
and I evade their stony presence
as well as the fresh waves
of condemnation,
regret about the food I ate
to add protective bulk
I did not need
but didn't know it.

All these stories of blame,
of choices I was blind to,
of ways I let my body down
and vice versa,
of ways I could have,
should have,
would have

and now this view
is just what is here,
rivulets of skin
like sand moved by shoreline,
rippling and visible.

Well met
old friend;
in this deep glance
I see how life
has traced your face
with strange sweetness,
how suffering
and success
have taught their different dances,
moved you
through your paces.

I am glad
to see joy in these lines,
relieved to see depth
in your scars,
room for us to talk
about the valleys
without fear.

Yours is not a mask;
a quick and open map
to accompany travel
– thank you
for this present journey.

She is not very clean
and has a glint in her eye
and stumbles up to me, angry.
You are all fucking morons!
more than a mutter,
less than a scream,
and I am so surprised
I stop to listen
and watch as she kneels
by a patch of berries,
some of which are bleeding.

She cradles the whole ones
and tries to place her body
as some protective shield,
a warning
to slow down,
to see how life glistens
and needs attention.

Her rage is alarming
like a fierce bell
clamouring,
a judgment on ignorance,
compelling my fall,
nose-deep in brilliance,
fragile.

Flags

I am still trying
to be the wind,
to puff behind your flag
as if I could extend it
to snap gently,
or temper its snapping
by applying less force

and while it irks
to see you hanging limp
on such a sunny day

I keep patching rips
in my own cloth.
I try to summon breeze
instead of enjoying
my own stillness,
feeling my colours sag,
knowing that my holes
will allow me to flutter
and not be destroyed
in future tempests.

Our flagpoles are planted
close enough
we sometimes touch
and slap,
admire each other's unfurling.

There is no wind
I can conjure,
no rivulet of air
at my command,
we flap and fly and fade
here in real weather.

The rain sounds cold
on my bare legs
under this roof

I am not hearing
just the moisture
on a lawn
with lips sprung wide
in satiated hope

or the way
each droplet
helps fill
unseen aquifers
under me and my neighbours

today I hear
the cold ripple,
imaginary caress
I am running from
so often

as if beaches are always warm

or sand never longs for raindrops

help me to listen
without quivering

to the wet we depend on.

I give me
permission
to be irresponsible

to delight in my freedom
and scamper through my days

to taste fully
and lick the contents of the bowl
even before the others
have a chance to

to let my grin
be the offering,
rather than something from this sack
I lug around

let me drop it here
to play
with open arms

understand how my own dancing
is plenty.

Detective

Drop the magnifying glass,
take off the gold star,
trenchcoat, false moustache,
comfortable old fedora

there are clues
but so much effort
to record them

to fidget them
into changing patterns

detective
this mystery
has no cold trail

the footprints you follow are yours

the warm sand beckons.

The safety pin

Somewhere in my middle
I have a very safe pin
holding all this stuff I hold

the pivot around which the shit could
fly,
keeping my shit together

and the more I say yes
the stronger the pin

because if the shit hits the fan
this could be a real mess.

And not just me,
because I have a backpack
and options for sprinting

but all these precious beloveds
I can't let fall.

The centripetal force
of all this spinning,
my solar plexus
wrapped like a loaded diaper,
the safety pin
protecting us all from the explosion
of a genuine flow.

Dinosaur eggs
in my belly
or maybe dragon
... some roiling creature
inside a cold rock,
a lump of resistance
protecting me
from monsters.

These belly stones
are my no,
my ego treasures,
stored against the day
when giving comes knocking,
when love invites me out to play.

And because my cool burdens
keep me inside,
love trickles slowly
through the roof,
entering the windows of my heart
to flood my basement,
warming the monsters,
listening as they claw against their
cages.

Soon they will set themselves free,
fangs and all,
wet wings ready to unfurl.

I have ideas
about joy,
like a yardstick
lugged with me,
invisible
but causing this slight limp

a burden
I am trying to leave behind.

The measuring interferes
with small flashes;
I miss the glints of light
when I am squinting
for the numbers,
neglect to see the tiny grins
and soft invitations.

Contentment sounds like compromise,
a used car
instead of ecstasy on offer

but I know I will go farther
in this model,
drop the high speed chasing
for this everyday journey,
listen to the music
of sputtering,
feel the ride
of a jerky transmission,
my teacher everywhere.

Maybe today
the U.N. will call
with that mission
in the refugee camps

or a long-lost friend
whose name only returns
when she speaks it

or some new soul
in need of contact

or maybe it will be the bank
asking for my opinion
or my overdraft

or someone prodding me
to keep a promise

there is something about uncertainty
I truly dread

and yet if I knew,
I'd feel so constricted

surely this whining
is not my true voice

and I can step away
from the phone.

What if the day of my funeral
rises so bright and rich with light
that no one comes to remember?

What if they go to the park
and think afterwards
there was something they meant to do?

What if I am the last to go
among my web of obligatory loves
except for a few who are travelling
and can't get home?

What if there are two or three
and food for twenty
and uncomfortable silence?

What if they have to stretch back
to my dusty awards in high school
for fleshing out a speech?
What if they don't bother?

My questions
scrape away fear
to find where humour lives
… I will never know these answers,
and despite the way they burn,
they don't matter.

Drop it
as if you are a dog
she said
and since that's exactly
what I have felt
I could hear my heart sing

and even these words
shake gently in my mouth,
a woof of repressed laughter,
slobbering on a bone
I can't quite set down

like this pen
that needs to scrawl
so something can be shared

even as my mouth opens
and the drool slides,
bone hitting toes,
a light space
where you are welcome
and I don't need
to sketch the door.

There are lesbians
who are strong in their joy
because of finding
who they are

and others of us
who know our need
for woman-love
because evolution is slow
and our men
cannot hold us
on their own.

And so it may take
a few more lifetimes
(or dozens or more)
before the yin and yang
can greet each other
swimming in natural circles of awe,
vortices of delight
in a river
where breathing keeps us moist,
where we spin around each other
and still journey downriver with ease.

Come unto me
for refreshment
for today I suck deeply
from an aquifer
that knows no end

it trusts in the earth
to filter salt
from the infinite ocean

and rises up fresh
for the giving.

Too long I worried
about the shape and weight
of my bucket

but today the well
is full to the brim

and you and you and you
can cup your hands.

I keep thinking
about a kind of freedom
like a skirt on a beach
and a satchel, with maybe one orange
and pen and paper

but find myself open
to this encumbered joy,
with all these loves and sorrows,
these purple petals,
the weight of all this building
I carry with me.

The birdsong moves me
through ears that are not empty,
bouncing off the echoes
of a busy mind.

So this is the song of my happiness,
how it moves through
all this poignant decomposing,
how there is room
for trilling and cawing
because both are here,
for waste and tenderness.

And even as I pity
my own story of burdens
I see the beach recede
like a veil lifted
and feel my true freedom
flickering now.

I am living
in my dying,
fragile and awake,
tender in the finitude
of my days.

Friends have gone
and some have not yet come
and my fear
of going too soon
is just pretend,
a clenched fist
that can open
with a tearful grin,
knowing the journey
is always too soon
and starts right now
or from my first breath.

Poems and sonatas
are never done,
medicine unfinished in a jar,
half a bag of earth filled,
kisses undelivered

there is no tidy ending,
let me embrace
the messy fragments now

let a larger
and more useless
whirlwind enter in
to shake what I have known
and watch the dust floating

to let this bile have room
for its empty loss
and then stop making more

to let a rising current
other than my will
lift these frail tubes of calcium
to greet a world
too heavy to carry

let me quiet enough
to hear one heartbeat
without the help of fingers

let me stop holding out
for a perfect death
or a perfect life,
open my palm to this one.

Two unwilling students
bound in learning,
entwined in listening to truths
we don't want to hear

two wise teachers
hiding from each other,
afraid to speak our wisdom
for fear of causing pain

two urgent lovers
scared of the calendar
and all its lessons
layered in time

surely we can trust
these flames arise
from logs that are more sturdy
than wax and wick.

Like a willful toddler
I am poised with this pen,
a permanent marker
ready to leave indelible scratches,
loving the idea
of a muse
to give me power and impunity

and like a true mother
she invites me
to show a little grace,
to hand up my weapon

watch her skillful hand.

Everyday Oracle

No steaming pool
or sacrifices,
no cave to provoke awe
or slippery slope
for entrance,
no following
or ads.

Just a willingness
to sit on this couch,
receiving calls
and other forms of listening,
watching
as bones shake and fall
in new patterns

feeling through entrails
otherwise ignored

knowing that light
shines on it all,
even dimly,

speaking
from warm shadows.

Greet the day
with the courage
to feel the ground under your feet
and bend softly
at the knees,
letting yourself fall gently
to an unseen chair.

Know that each day
the chair is different;
sometimes a broad sofa,
sometimes a tippy folding chair
requiring some balance;
occasionally
the rough embrace of dirt
under your bum,
a surprising view of sky.

I am almost done
with planning
where the chairs will go,
how to line them up
for my efficient use of life;

the day will carry me
without effort,
I am brave enough
to fall.

Time to wake my guru,
prod him out of bed
with affection
and coffee

to hear his groans
on rising

to await his instructions
on real love
and healthy sacrifice

and gorgeous greedy joy
freely shared.

Daisy

Intricate brown
at the centre
of my soul,
a warm round
encircling my core,
fulfilling belly.

Like a graceful tutu
glistening,
each bright petal
is strongly connected,
fed by fluid
inducted from earth
and rising.

Implicit in petal
the falling away,
but now
the shining,
even as I cannot
own them,
feeding what will float.

Simple and supple,
blooming.

My song of freedom
has sounded too long
like a croak
or a quaver
and I hear now
all the echoes
of fear that is not mine.

I hear the voices
whispered in the dark
of women
who were so afraid
of triggering violence,
who walked delicately
on eggshells
all the time

who longed for boldness
seen in their crazy neighbours
and understood their own tears
as the flames met flesh and hair.

And the walls
around perfumed gardens
where women whisper
and silks rustle
and there are swords
and rough sacks
for journeys outside.

And the many homes
where TV remotes
are briefly dropped
to swat and swing
and imprint knuckles

on soft skin,
a deep branding.

And so this voice
that is my own
and this pen I briefly borrow
rejoice
in the warble of freedom,
in the safety of a home
where the lion
has a deep purr
and even his roaring is melody,
where the fear
can creep out safely
to be warmed,
where the huntress
can find her friends
and fierce shared power
to feed her family,
offerings for a silenced choir.

I spoke
from my true heart,
the one that shines
even when I don't,
the ageless warm

and when you raged
your book on the floor
hurled in my direction

there was surprise,
an unexpected rift.

But this is the gift
of substantive work,
the slap
that says transforming
is underway,
two steps back,
signifying progress.

Praise is the softer touch,
criticism and hostility
more true,
reliable in their signals.
Onwards
we shine brighter
as the fittings are walloped,
coal revealing diamond
under pressure.

Surrendered pen,
I just hand it over
and the sloppy marks
dance with precision
and her love trickles
onto the page
and there is fun here too.

I never promised
just sunshine
says the grey sky
and the rain has not yet come
but the clouds
protect this green
from too much heat

and we have lived
for aeons
in this bubble of water and air
with all the billions
of adjustments
so we are tended daily

and surely this constant care
will soothe our greed
so a more delicate grace
will lighten our footprints,
the bubble keep spinning
its sloshy cargo.

Give me precision,
a surgeon with a gentle knife,
sharp to separating
wisdom and arrogance.

Help me to feel where the muscles
that relax into knowing
are different
from the clench of certainty

how my theories
cause harm

how there is water
in my outstretched hand
and it may not be the fox
who comes to lick it.

Give me a fine needle,
strong thin fibre
a wise gaze
for stitching my own wounds,
a refraining hand
where lancing lets blood flow.

Earthbag 2014

It is a wall
made with love,
encircling an empty space
that may house more love...

friendships as hands
filling cans of earth
filling bags designed for seeds
for a solid planting

settling and rising,
walls with holes
for windows and doors
and space for future journeys

look at all these faces
smiling under dust,
wet gravel transforming
in strong gifts on offer.

Vertebrae

This spine can curve
and twist and flex
even with all these layers
of stacked bones

the way we let life
spill through the channel
of our stacked days

body food money
sensation sex union
family friends phone calls
ego imagination yearning
love gratitude welcoming
creating asking listening
seeing planning transforming

with Gaia's fluid
nurturing our sanity
nourishing structural integrity,
cherished resilience.

Rain this morning
washing plans
past just soggy
until disintegration

the clean plate,
empty bowl

vitality pouring
like soup outside the dish,
ladles of love
floating a white tureen

a backwards appreciation
for the scent of empty space
wafting through all this flavour.

Rain last night
and now a thin line
of sunlight over mountains
promising nothing

clouds still thick,
lawn wet
and lying exposed
for more to come,
water or wind or sun.

All this looking for portents
to guide my steps
just makes me crane my gaze,
a pain in the neck;

the clouds will pulse
without my help,
rain and sun
fall where they will.

The river flows north
at the end of my road
all the time

not just when I remember
or when summer melts the ice

but as constant
as anything can be
on a human scale.

Today my son and I
rode bikes to see it,
a minor journey
well worth the effort.

Sun and sage
and fish only visible
when they jumped for food

and clouds that looked like meditating
dragons
or ladies with rays in their heads

my belly caressed by ground…

that river murmurs always

my visits rare
and cherished.

The universe
throws up her hands sometimes,
a mother with a teen,
frustrated by my pace.

Wishing I could taste and see
instead of sulk,
or act defiant
or slog like this, head down,
determined to protect my story.

The life force
dances with a pan of sweets,
trying to entice me awake,
a sudden shake
in the leaves rippling
right in plain view.

She needs real people,
vibrant vessels for her light,
her salty syrup,
live ones
willing to be poured
as they are, genuine.

And even as I slog,
I sometimes catch her eye
to share a wink
and we both know
this rebellion
won't last.

My third chakra
is screaming,
I can only hear the noise
and feel the pressure

like a tantrum out of control

and I don't know what it wants

or how I should make change

but somewhere I am mad as hell
and have a fire
building steam with no direction
like a train parked
disconnected from its own wheels
and off the rails.

Less and more and less and more
I keep feeding fuel
to an oven that needs less heat
or more travel,
less waiting or more lubrication,
some way for steam
to carry me forward,
calm and present
in a carriage with the vista in flux,
moving always.

I want to fall in love,
want to be someone new
who falls in love
and stays that way
all the time.

I know of a woman
who wants to sell
and head off on adventures
unnamed

and a man
who would go with her
if it seemed
like there was any point

and my body
is too present
with all the ways I am grateful
to let me cry real tears

but I do feel
something
as I pinch these wilting pansies,
even though they are still lovely
sapping strength from new growth
needing to be trimmed.

Metaphors fall like rain
and drip into ponds
where we glimpse their beauty
or ugly teachings
and think they are pebbles

oh gentle reader
with your aches and aversions
and secret joys

just keep holding out
palms flat in receiving

let them be stages
for marvels

watch the steady evaporation
as beauty dissolves,
carried by wind
towards a new landing.

Register

Subservient
to my own wisdom
and resisting
the dominance of my ideas

she calls forth
an obedience
I can trust

even as my mind
falls away
to the edges of a vortex

making a hole
where I empty am

listening to a music
with no words
and few sounds

noting a register

where I am humbled
and honouring

fully here and gone.

My humble experience
is that new growth
happens less often through doorways
and more frequently
by falling down a hole
I did not see coming.

Or just a good twist
of my ankle,
a hard thump on the ground
to lie dazed
in a new perspective.

The safety police
in my own soul
work very hard
to avoid these hazards.

But sometimes,
when they are confident they've done
well
they doze a little
and I have room to sneak free
to hear whatever words
I don't want to say.

Foreboding

Insomnia and shifting hormones
are tidy words
to wrap around this cold dread,
the slow creep of doom
siding up my belly
to wash my gaze with sadness

so that every glance
has the colour of despair,
regret for how the focus is blurry,

the promise of sweetness
so badly out of alignment.

All my loves
tinged with pain,
smiles like grimaces
or even the ones
who show deep resilience
don't see how the bounce awaits,
how their joy will also crash

how this foreboding
feels like a surgeon's lamp
exposing a putrid realness.

Topics flutter
like addicted moths
circling the lamp

my desolate finances,
the snap and hiss of friendship,
a gross of extinctions
caused by our greed,

the soft sleepiness
of our constant reach for more

a light in dark night
not for soothing welcome,
a harsh interrogation;

the best I can hope for
is a limp nod
from other exhausted survivors.

I felt the rough flick
of your dragon tail
spreading unconscious cold
and knocking things
behind you

for too long
I felt like the princess
imprisoned
by hot breath
and cold scales

lately I have been seeing
the trail of my own lizard length,
debris and smoke stains
I was blind to,

feeling my own
claws and wings.

We dragons
afraid of our own flames
have skulked in this cave
for decades

afraid of the burning.

Help us to learn to roar,
to fly in new bright,
to flame where heat is called for,
to nestle at end of day,
curled tails entwining.

I paddle
in a leaky boat
in a broad deep ocean.

Although I am afraid of cold,
mostly I know
how the ocean carries,
how it absorbs
the small me,
invisible plankton
nourishing immensity.

I thought this was a poem
about patching holes,
learning how to sail,
finding more freedom.

Instead
I touch cold salty wet

seeping through my defenses,
reminder of how briefly I float
and all the creatures
pulsing unseen below waves.

Pen hovers over page
like waiting on the surface of a pond,
tracing lines and circles
briefly noticed,
rippling and gone.

Heart moves the same,
learning lessons
that trickle
or splash
or drip like liquid salt
and slide away.

Joy is in the breath
of making space,
allowing pointless purpose
to run free,
making friends with dread
and all the other voices,
feeling how music
is only heard
one time.

I don't like to make room
for dread,
the way its cold fingers
grip my worldview,
my belly cold and clammy.

It strips the world skeletal,
stark bones
with no comfort.

It slaps the poignant warmth
from each breath,
dulling each thought
with sticky gloom.

Today's sunrise
looked like a symphony of salmon,
flashing scales and sheets of golden
notes
draped in air
before the clouds
consolidated drenching
to make light invisible.

All that happened
was a cloud dance took over,
pregnant with rain
and labouring;

the symphony continues unseen,
a marvel in other time zones.

Synthesis

Some cooks
wrap meat
in pastry.

Some painters
mix dark and light
to blend new shades.

I take truths
like hot and cold
and craft them,
warm abiding.

Many women
share this courage,
embracing the cold
even as its fingers
trail starkly.

We have learned
to be cautious,
feeling how men
grasp the life-ring,
trying to escape the ocean

even as both
swell together.

And while caution
brings its own regret,
its realness
brings more synthesis.

Bag Lady

My unconscious works hard at night,
sweeping up worries,
jumbling the images I've collected,
trying to sort the recycling,
make a little beauty from my trash.

In the morning
I wash off the residue
of yesterday's sorrow,
forgive the broken glass,
let water sluice
for any bits of treasure.

I greet the day
briefly naked,
ready to be touched
by what is here,
ready to walk the street
with an empty cart,
a loose sack available
on my shoulder.

Aimless, yes,
but willing to let one foot
prompt the other,
to leave the home and map,
gather what finds me.

Living in the woods,
I don't have a curb
to drag things out to
but I still rummage
in the basement,
finding old pieces
I am afraid to love,
dusty objects of my inattention,
junk that might have been precious
or rusty knives.

I am getting stronger
as I haul stuff outside,
debris that seems fragile
in sun and wind

finding my sources of kindness
like water from ground,
aiming the hose
with gentle precision,
washing useless ornaments
in case someone wants them,
making more space inside.

Credit card bills
and drying plants
and bits of mold
on wasted berries

… I keep grasping
for a consummate tonglen,
an in-breath
of pain and noticing
transformed by love
so that the next gasp
is painless.

Instead this dance,
detritus and seeds,
decay nor growth winning,
a spectrum of light and shadow,
a tiptoe of brief balance,
flickering.

We sat on a loveseat,
a sofa, one leather rocker
and two on the carpet
politely listening

the dark one was black that night
and barely there, like a cool shadow

the bright one was sick
and out of tune, chattering to rock

the otters rolled together on the floor,
puzzled by their own attendance

and I who had summoned the circle,
an oracle lost in translation,
could only taste disappointment,
a tree-nymph banging silently
on the underside of bark,
unheard except as slight vibration
in crowning leaves
too high above the forest floor.

Invitation unspoken,
no blame for their deafness,
no regret, and shame can be let go
as wisdom smiles.
Forceful yearning in my imprisoning
tree,
the pounding of my fistful heart
shook invisible pollen,
floating from above,
landing into time,
fragrant hidden orchids
budding and starting to bloom
in an unseen, tended circle.

These yawns are part of it,
the slow awakening
with sleepy-headed sloth
and resting on this couch,
bumbling along in my journey
to alertness,
a wakeful happiness dangling
like a musical mobile
to amuse this tired child.

These names no longer stir me,
epithets of laziness,
my weak character
finding small patches of grass
on which to lie in the sun
and tune out exhortations.

Tone is everything
… I hope you can hear
how the scathing has grown softer,
how this armchair activist
is genuinely grateful
for this particular warm upholstery.

Ceyote

I'm a slow learner
and keep forgetting
that your wounds
are not for healing

not for fixing
so we journey neatly forward

my wisdom is impatient
and wants you free
from the story of your pain

but my love
is wiser still
and knows deep holes
are wonderful
for stumbling
into hidden pools of grace.

She carries a torch for him;
down through the ages
they have passed it
hand to hand,
sometimes she struggles
to lift it high,
one hand on the skirt,
sometimes he wields it
with valour
while she moves in flickering shadow
behind.

This time,
that one time,
she walks with it flaming
and leads through passages
that feel cold and dark,
a fierce protective light
in hallways of dread,
exposing the glittering eyes

bravely calling forth monsters
to duel or dance,
seeing their hunger
and how their scales glisten,
how delicate and strong
their hidden wings.

It all looks so calm
and yet this churning
is barely viable;
I feel sucked in
to my own vortex
and I'd rather escape

but here is the quaver,
the way-too-much
of this urgent call
to run in ten directions

fighting for control
and for surrender
all at once

not knowing how to stay
and let fall
and trust my apathy too

this path is unpleasant;
am trying to stay with the truth
of this vertigo,
the nausea of this spin.

Rescue is coming
but not from outside
or even inside,

a future landing
when this cycle
spins itself out.

By reaching in
to touch my own jealousy
and the soft band around my ribs
I have known like a large manacle

it seems my oppression
has carried me
like a rubber ring in ocean,
a floatie
holding me safe in waves.

Now I am growing large
and its soft pressure
constricts more than lifts
and it is the season
to remove it
but I don't know how.

A season to settle now
into my own enlightenment,
lightening my load
with a natural buoyancy,
knowing I can swim
and let drowning touch me,
knowing this cheap plastic is useless,
knowing I will splutter and feel salt,
that dolphins and sea otters
will teach me to glide.

Tomorrow

You keep saying
you don't want to get old,
don't want to feel the pain
of limitation,
don't want to let the shame
of weakness and confusion
shape your days.

It appeals to you,
this idea of a fiery crash
or chosen end,
the illusion of control,
a tidy finish.

And makes me mad,
even as I make room
for hearing your story
without judgment,
here on this creative edge
where judgment dangles anyway...

I don't understand
why the pain caused by holding up
all these protections,
burning with this constant acid,
is preferable
to a pain that might never come.

We all have our projects:
some plot meals to share with friends,
some watch their investments daily
or even more often,
or let fear niggle at constant debt;
some buy paint and canvas
for nighttime raids on their own
imagination.

Planting, building,
spending time on boards
(as groups or planks),
cycling for a race,
standing in line for water,
checking Facebook,
learning to juggle...

waking from sleep,
we can let our projects
feed us now.

My people,
these mostly-whites,
slightly tired
from all the effort,
paying for seats
from which to watch the show,
the flow of fire
hinting at tears,
drawing inspired breath.

Steady, they hold space
for other lives,
breed community
with their patience,
pass quiet torches
in everyday hands.

I never thought I'd use a cane
and maybe I won't
but that hobble
reminds me of my own family
and all the ways I move.

Vapour

Love spills
into hearts
open to decency,
to planted standing
on sacred and familiar ground

not swayed by fame
or accolades
but soaking into real roots,
tender and gnarled passages.

Sometimes it drips
into aquifers
where others lift it up
with no thread back
to where it came from,
love as replenishing nectar.

Sometimes earth will carry it to sea,
capillaries of streams and rivers
moving it onwards,
nourishing where it touches shore,
gathering momentum.

Our dry spells
give us gifts
of evaporation,
essential for new rain.

We were so young
when we started sharing
stories of the world

I was raised with butterflies
and you with turnips and pigs
 - one crawling and flying,
and two kinds of rooting.

In the early days
I showed you colour flitting by
and you snorted
and I learned to look
more closely at the ground.

Later the wings
kept brushing my face
and landing in my hair
and I felt sad
you couldn't see them.

Now we sit
in the warm dirt
under a sun
that holds us in orbit,
united and distinct,
like everything.

The tired face
of God
has a softer glow
than bright halo

lined and gentle
beyond resignation,
having given up
with open hands
all these galaxies
to spin on their own

knowing
both rise and fall
and beauty in them

smiling
without a sermon
or even much hope,
having invented smiles.

Litany

There was a time
when call and response
made sense,
when rhythm was known
and people knew their place
and words were honoured
even in rote.

Now all these soundings
confuse the whales
and we stagger too,
listening for truth
and croaking our unpracticed reply.

Courage still carries;
that heartfelt fear
made sturdy,
the tentative start
to singing
barely more than whispers
as we join in new music.

Fleeting and unique,

these songs are treasured

in dissipation,

rainbows catching light

during one fine mist,

gorgeous echoes fading

when mouths close.

No words for this
body,

memories loosely strung

on flowing wires,

discomfort and pleasure

stretched

on a network of time.

Not the wires

or feelings,

not sensation or data,

there is a white puff

briefly

more distant and more loving

than a sigh.

I could use this time
to clean my cupboards
and that would be just fine
… no poem
but less chaos
when that door is opened.

Better and worse
have pinioned my wings
for so long,
feathers fluttering
without flight.

Action is precious,
stillness or movement,
useless and sublime
no matter the choice.

Wake me
to more honey beads
of serendipity,
the sweet convergence
where secret jokes
come to life
at the hub,
moments tasted
for their once-and-only
even when they make great stories
later

impossible
made real

coincidence
lining up the players
to walk on that one street
for that one pause.

I know I have shuffled blindly
past saviours and friends,
disguised in plain view

but my greed has a pure desire;
let me wake to more miracles
in these ordinary days,
pull degrees of separation
in a tighter spin,
relishing.

Ablution

Let me wash my hands
close to the sensitive eye
that notices motion,
dancing my fingers lightly
without touch or forcing
until flow is released.

May I briefly feel
how I am in the right place
to access water,
moving my hands
to tend and receive,
letting myself be washed
and renewed
as a simple and everyday
supplication.

May I come to know
that water is waiting,
return with my layers of grit
inevitably gathered
to flutter and settle
in a font
where light can sense
receptivity.

May I value my own dirt,
the residue and unseen germs
that bring me daily
to this tap
with open palms.

www.ingramcontent.com/pod-product-compliance
Lightning Source LLC
Chambersburg PA
CBHW061753020426
42331CB00006B/1459